STRANGE SERIES

Book #2:

The Creepiest Places
in the World

Terrance Zepke

The Creepiest Places in the World

Safari Publishing

All queries should be directed to www.safaripublishing.net.

For more about this author, visit www.terrancezepke.com.

Library of Congress Cataloging-in-Publication Data

Zepke, Terrance

STRANGE SERIES: The Creepiest Places in the World

ISBN: 9781942738794

Terrance Zepke p. cm.

1. Creepy Places-World. 2. Occult. 3. Scary places. 4. Travel-World. 5. Oddities-Travel. 6. Nonfiction-Travel. 7. Special Interest Travel. 8. Supernatural. 9. Strange-World. I. Title.

First edition

10 9 8 7 6 5 4 3 2 1

CONTENTS

INTRODUCTION

Welcome to book two of my STRANGE SERIES. If you are interested in the mysterious, creepy, and downright strange, you will love this series!

Although I have written many books about the paranormal, I want to be clear that this is not a book about haunted places. There is a difference between a place being creepy and being haunted. Synonyms for "creepy" are *eerie, frightful, sinister, disturbing, spooky, ominous, ghoulish, kooky, gruesome, macabre, scary, disgusting and nasty.*

Some of the places discussed (like Gomantong Caves and Akodessawa Fetish Market) are eerie and disgusting. Other places (like the Ghost Church and Pripyat) are disturbing. Still others (like the Museum of Vampires & Legendary Creatures and The Clown Motel) are kooky. A few places (like Aokigahara Forest and Death Island) are sinister. I consider some to be macabre (like Haw Par Villa and the Torture

Museum). But the perfect word to sum them all up is creepy!

But it just so happens that some of these creepy places also happen to be haunted. Some of these places are abandoned, some are rundown and dilapidated, some are open to tourists and some are not, and some are easily accessible and others are not. Some have well-documented histories and some do not.

This book is meant to be a fun read, which means you shouldn't take any of its contents too seriously. I did my due diligence with research, but some of these stories are impossible to substantiate. And some are so ludicrous they can't be true, right? But they say that truth is stranger than fiction, so who knows?

So read on to discover the creepiest places in the world and prepare to be creeped out—but in a good way!

P.S. I have included a chapter from one of my most popular books, *Spookiest Objects,* at the back of the book that I think you will enjoy.

CITY OF THE DEAD (Russia)

Dubbed the *"City of the Dead,"* the Russian
village of Dargavs is considered to be one of the
creepiest places in Russia. Tucked away deep in
the Caucasus Mountains near the Georgia-
Russia border, Dargavs has a population of 100
or so tombs and no people.

These strange-looking stone tombs date
back to the 14th-century. They may resemble
village huts, but they were built to accommodate
the deceased. They also "house" all the personal
possessions that relatives chose to bury with
their loved ones.

It is said that this necropolis is cursed.

Anyone who dares to walk into it—who is not there to pay their respects to a loved one—will not live long. This may be something the locals made up to discourage tourists, but then again it may be true since locals (who do not have ancestors entombed here) will not enter the City of the Dead.

The crypts vary in size from tiny to four stories. The bigger crypts most likely belonged to bigger families. Some have curving roofs and windows, while others have no roofs or windows. Some even contain underground chambers.

Historians have a much darker take on how these structures came to be. A plague hit the area sometime between the 16th and 18th century AD that claimed thousands of lives. Historians believe that the afflicted and all his or her family members were sent to recover or die inside these pre-built crypts. They survived on whatever food locals brought and left outside the crypts. When they died from the plague (very few people survived the plague), their corpses were left to rot inside the huts.

Small wells have been dug in front of all of the crypts, which supports the historians' theory. After all, the deceased don't need water. If they had been buried in the crypts after their deaths, the wells wouldn't have been needed. Coins have been found in the bottom of the wells. According to legend, if loved ones dropped a coin into it and heard it hit the bottom of the well, it meant the deceased had made it to heaven.

Another theory suggests that the City of

the Dead was based on the Sarmatian tradition of burying the dead above ground to respect the land.

At one time, there was a watch tower in the necropolis. It is speculated that the tower was used to stand watch over the dead. Or if the theory about the plague victims being sent here is true, guards kept watch to make sure no one left the City of the Dead.

It is creepy to think that these poor plague victims were forced to live in their own graves until they succumbed to death and that their families had to go into the crypts as well, whether they had the plague or not. This would presumably have been family members living in the same household and not all living relatives.

Of course, this is just one theory and may not even be true. We may never know the origin of the City of the Dead or what brought these people to settle in this remote, harsh habitat, or if there is any truth to the curse.

Dargavs is in the republic of North Ossetia in southern Russia. To get there, you must journey for three hours along a dangerous, winding mountain road.

 **FYI: The City of the Dead contains roughly 100 ancient stone crypts spread out over 3.5 acres. These crypts hold the remains of more than 10,000 people.**

Nearby… in the foothills of the Caucasus mountains are Giant Stone Head Sculptures. Often referred to as the Easter Island of Georgia," the site contains a half dozen monolithic heads carved from granite. The sculptures are the work of artist Merab Piranishvili. His first (and also the largest sculpture) is a portrait of St. George. It was completed in 1984. The giant stone heads depict a different figure from Georgian history. Each head is carved from a single block of granite. Piranishvili's goal is to carve 500 heads for his free, open-air museum in Sno, which also is home to the 16th century Sno Castle.

PARIS UNDERGROUND (France)

Far below one of the most glamorous cities in the world lies a not-so-glamorous labyrinth of skulls and bones known as Les Catacombes. Extending for more than two hundred miles is a series of tunnels literally constructed of skeletal remains.

The catacombs were built in the 18th century when the graveyards throughout Paris ran out of room for the dead. This resulted in improper burials, mass graves, and the dead becoming the "undead" when their coffins popped up out of the earth. This was obviously a public health issue and also a smelly problem, as well.

City officials came up with a creative solution to bury bodies underground in the old quarry. So, beginning in 1786, bodies were dug up one by one and moved to the new, underground burial chamber. After the French Revolution, all bodies went directly to the catacombs for burial. During WWII, the Resistance used parts of the Catacombs as a hideout. Reportedly, the Nazis also used the Catacombs as bunkers.

A man named Louis Etienne Hericart took responsibility for creating the Catacombs. He arranged the skulls and bones as if creating an elaborate art project. Approximately six and million French citizens have been buried in these ossuaries.

The depth of the Paris Catacombs is equivalent to a five-story building. Visitors must descend 130 steps to reach them. It stays a consistent 57∘F (14∘C). Only part of the labyrinth is open to the public, the area known as Denfert-Rochereau.

During the $17 - 20^{th}$ centuries, the old quarry was used as a distillery. Beer was brewed due to ideal temperatures and brewing conditions. More secret caves were allegedly dug by the breweries. One brewery, Dumesnil, stayed in operation until the 1960s.

The catacombs have been a popular tourist attraction since 1874. Even royalty has succumbed to morbid curiosity. Charles X, Francis I, and the Ladies of the Court have descended into the dark depths of the city's underground to glimpse the ossuary. Napoleon III brought his son to Paris to see the world famous underground cemetery.

Over the years, the ossuary has been

17

renovated numerous times to add steps, lights, vaults, and support walls. There are many miles of tunnels that are off limits to visitors. In fact, there are large portions of the tunnels that have never been mapped. Some folks who have sneaked in afterhours have gotten lost and died in the Catacombs. How ironic!

What makes this place creepy is not necessarily the millions of bones and skulls on display but the labyrinth itself. It is no surprise that a place known as "The World's Largest Grave" is also one of the most haunted places in the world.

Some people have slipped into one of the

many secret entrances to practice necromancy. Necromancy is a practice of magic involving communication with the deceased – either by summoning their spirit as an apparition or raising them bodily. This is done for the purpose of divination, imparting the means to foretell future events or discovering hidden knowledge, or to bring someone back from the dead. Ritual participants used body parts to practice as part of their ceremonies and it is rumored that drugs and sacrifices were involved.

There is a group of people known as 'cataphiles' who live undetected in a remote part of the Catacombs. This may not seem possible but given that the tunnels extend more than 200 miles with much of it not even mapped, one can see how it is not only possible, but highly probable. So if Parisian officials do not even know about these tunnels, how did these cataphiles find them?

It is believed that a secret entrance was discovered many years ago by a group of explorers. That led to being able to access the Catacombs freely. This unlimited exploration led to the discovery of previously unknown sections of tunnels and more secret entrances. Eventually, some cataphiles began living in the Catacombs. It is rumored that there are dozens of rooms in a secret section of the Catacombs that have been made into apartments. There is a large, communal space that has been converted into an underground night club!

As you can imagine, this is not all that peaceful for eternal slumber. Spirits have been continually disturbed and disrespected, so it is not surprising that paranormal activity has been abundant over the years.

Many visitors swear they have been touched by an unseen presence. Flashlights with fresh batteries often malfunction in the catacombs. Shadowy figures are seen briefly before disappearing. Visitors report having felt they were being watched and followed. Cold spots have suddenly and inexplicably been experienced in a place that otherwise has a consistent temperature of 57∘F/14∘C. Ghost hunters have recorded mysterious EVPs and images.

One well known ghost hunting group that has investigated the Catacombs is Travel Channel's *Ghost Adventures*. They recorded all kinds of strange stuff, including a luminous spirit walking past one of their cameras.

Some visitors have experienced hysterical breakdowns and a few claim that an unseen force tried to strangle them. Since some people have actually died in the Catacombs, it is easy to see how their spirits may not be at peace.

One such spirit may belong to Philibert Aspairt, who went into the Catacombs and never came out. It is believed he got lost while exploring and died before he could find his way out. His corpse was eventually discovered not far from an exit. It is believed that his spirit still roams the Catacombs to this day, possibly still searching for a way out.

An examination of his video equipment reveals that Aspairt was last filmed taping the Catacombs before dropping his camera and running away in fear. Heavy breathing and the sounds of running are heard until the footsteps are too far away to hear anymore—and then the camera's batteries go dead. What frightened him so badly that he took off running? Did he get lost trying to escape or did something more sinister occur? We'll never know since Aspairt never made it out of this massive morbid maze to share his story.

It is believed that dozens more have gotten lost and died while illegally exploring this vast underground tunnel system.

Perhaps these explorers should have paid closer attention to the entrance sign, which reads:

"Arrete, c'est ici l'empire de la mort!"
(Stop! This is the empire of death!)

The Catacombs are part of the History of Paris Museum. There is a 45-minute tour that anyone can take for a small fee. French, German, Spanish, and English-speaking guides are available. Children under the age of 14 must be accompanied by a parent. The tour includes nearly 1.5 miles (2.2 km) of walking.

According to rumors, Cataphiles offer illegal tours. If you are inclined to explore illegally on your own, you should do so with a cataphile because they know the tunnels better than anyone.

Also according to rumors, a private, secret party was held in the catacombs on July 16, 2022. Invitees were sent a link and a password to a survey form. If you were chosen, you were told the meeting spot on the day of the party. One partygoer turned on her fitness tracker and found she had traveled four and a half miles underground. The route ultimately led her to a large central cave, where there was a DJ, a bar with neon lights, candles, and people dancing.

1, Avenue du Colonel Henri Rol-Tanguy - 75014 Paris, France
http://www.catacombes.paris.fr/en/homepage-catacombs-official-website

A helpful brochure that you can print out detailing the route and sights of this tour is available at
http://www.catacombes.paris.fr/sites/catacombes/files/editeur/pm_catacombes_depliant_gb.pdf

More Creepy, Spooky or Just Plain Weird Things to Do in Paris

The Crypt at the historic Pantheon monument houses many famous French people. http://www.paris-pantheon.fr/en

Dans le Noir is not necessarily scary but it is strange. Lunch and dinner are served in pitch black with little information provided about the dishes being served. The idea is that by limiting your sense of sight, other senses are intensified and the dining experience is elevated. You definitely need to be an adventurous eater to be up for this experience! https://paris.danslenoir.com/en/

Ghosts, Mysteries & Legends Night Walking Tour reveals the biggest murders, executions, plagues, and wars that have rocked this capital city. The two-hour guided tour starts at Pont Neuf and finishes at Hotel de Ville. During the tour, you will see many of the city's famous landmarks and hidden treasures, as well as hear some spine-chilling stories. https://www.tripadvisor.com/AttractionProductReview-g187147-d11449787-Ghosts_Mysteries_and_Legends_Night_Walking_Tour_of_Paris-Paris_Ile_de_France.html

Immersive Live Thriller. Actively participate in a live police investigation staged in the center of Paris, which may include exploring abandoned basements, analyzing crime scenes, interrogating a suspect, or taking part in surveillance as you hunt down a mysterious serial killer. Guided by professional actors you will face various scenarios leading you to one of four possible outcomes. The experience lasts over two hours and is designed for groups of two to six people. https://borderliveconcepts.com/en/thelivethriller/

Musée des Égouts is a sewer tour, but it is also a unique way to discover the city's history and see Paris from a different perspective. The underground passages are dark, narrow, and creepy. The museum is located inside the sewer system, so it is damp and a bit smelly. https://en.parisinfo.com/paris-museum-monument/71499/Musee-des-egouts-de-Paris

Museum of Magic is a private museum full of antique magic props, optical illusions, and other curiosities. Wizard guides will share the history of magic and the world of illusion. The tour ends with a magic show. During the summer, magic classes are offered for children and there are year-round workshops. https://www.museedelamagie.com

Paris Manor is a cross between a haunted house and museum. Each room of the house is dedicated to a different legend brought to life with props, music, sound effects, and actors. Manoir de Paris offers an escape room, as well. http://www.lemanoirdeparis.com

THE BONE CHURCH (Czech Republic)

I didn't think I would ever describe a church as creepy but the Ossuary Church (a.k.a. "The Church of Bones") is the exception. This Gothic chapel, located in the basement of the Cemetery Church of All Saints, is home to the skulls and bones of more than 40,000 people.

We're not talking buried inside a coffin, tomb, or mausoleum. Thousands and thousands and thousands of bones and skulls are literally on full display throughout the church. They are everywhere! These body parts belong to people who believed that being enshrined in this church would result in a quick ascension to the afterlife.

The old bones have been transformed into chandeliers, candleholders, and buntings. Garlands of skulls have been strung across the ceiling and displayed in other highly creative ways.

The macabre artwork draws more than 200,000 visitors a year, making it one of the most popular tourist attractions in the Czech Republic.

In 1870, a woodcarver named Frantisek Rint was appointed to excavate and organize all these skeletal remains. What he came up with is not something you expect to find in a church chapel.

This underground chapel contains a massive chandelier made entirely of bones, as well as dozens of garlands of human skulls. Also, a collection of human skulls is piled on top of one another, resembling a gigantic tiki pole. The largest collection of bones have been arranged in four bell-shaped mounds that occupy each corner of the chapel. Recently, more skeletons were discovered in unmarked graves during a renovation project.

It has been dubbed the Church of Bones or the Bone Church, but it is officially known as the Cemetery Church of All Saints with Ossuary. At one time, it was part of the Sedlec monastery.

The church was built in the 14th century, and according to legend, one of the local abbots brought soil from Jerusalem and scattered it around the cemetery making it the oldest so-called "holy field" in Central Europe. https://www.sedlec.info/en/

CHAUCHILLA CEMETERY (Peru)

This is not your typical cemetery. Located roughly twenty miles south of Nazca, the cemetery was a well-kept secret from 200 AD until its discovery in the 1920s.

The Nazca prepared their dead for their journey to the afterlife. Yes, we're talking *mummified*. Because of the dry climate of the Peruvian desert, the mummies are remarkably well preserved. There is hair, teeth, and even skin on many of them. They are dressed in their best clothes for their journey to the afterlife. Much of the clothing is still intact and the bodies have been painted with a resin to preserve them.

This kept the bodies fairly safe from insects and bacteria that normally feeds on decomposing bodies. The tombs are made out of mud bricks, which not only housed these mummies but helped preserve them, as well.

Due to relentless grave robbing, the cemetery is now protected by the Peruvian government. Tourists may tour the sacred and protected site for a fee. If you go, you will find the dozens of skulls randomly scattered around the cemetery to be a spectacularly creepy sight. The origin of these heads is unknown.

You can go on your own or hire a day guide in Nazca. To get to the cemetery, take 1S/Pan American Highway south out of Nazca (19 miles/30kilometers) to the Carretera a Chauchilla and look for signs. Wear sunscreen and bring water if you go.

FYI: This cemetery was used in a scene from the blockbuster movie, *Indiana Jones and the Kingdom of the Crystal Skull.*

ISLAND OF THE DOLLS (Mexico)

Mexico City is comprised of sixteen municipalities, which includes Xochimilco ("Place of Flowers"). Situated on the southern shore of Lake Xochimilco, Xochimilco is best known for its complex canal system.

The canals, along with many little islands called chinampas, are a tourist draw. Visitors enjoy mariachi music, food, and drinks during a leisurely two-hour boat ride.

Gondola-style boats, known as trajineras, are well-suited to navigate the picturesque lake, canals, and manmade islands. These islands serve as floating gardens, created by the Aztecs to feed the residents of the ancient city of Tenochititlan. Critical to this ecosystem are the native juniper trees known as ahuejotes. There is concern that too much tourism is harming these trees, thereby threatening the entire ecosystem of this area, which became a UNESCO World Heritage Site in 1987.

During the time of Cortez, many people fled to Xochimilco and hid on the canals. Many were women and children who were hiding from the conquistadores. Most of the women killed themselves rather than be caught and raped by the Spanish. Later, the island was also used as shelter for Mexican revolutionaries and religious practitioners who may have fallen out of favor. It was used as a hideout; a place to disappear.

Nowadays, it is known as the Island of the Dolls because of a tragic story involving a little girl who drowned here in 1950. Her small corpse was found by a local farmer, Don Julian Santana Barrera, near La Isla de las Muñecas. The dead child was still clinging to her favorite baby doll.

At one time, the island had dozens of inhabitants. But by the 1950s, most people had moved off the island. It soon became a forgotten island. But Don Julian Santana Barrera stayed on the island because it was the only home he had ever known.

Barrera remained haunted and traumatized at the sight of the dead little girl he found. He saw her when he tried to sleep. He thought about her when he was awake. He became obsessed with her. He claimed she spoke to him, sharing her tragic tale and asking for more dolls to play with.

According to legend, she told Barrera that she had been playing with two other little girls when she fell into the water and drowned. She also told him that more dolls were needed to ward off evil spirits that were trying to take hold of the island and anyone on it. She told him that evil spirits wandered these wetlands and they must be appeased or else bad things would happen.

Barrera was convinced the spirit of the little girl had taken possession of her doll and that there was a real threat from evil, so he hung a doll from a tree to appease her spirit. As he came across more dolls, he hung those too. He once confessed that he had seen these dolls come alive at night. He said that they move their little heads and whisper to one another. He admitted he was frightened at first, but got used to it.

Barrera collected discarded doll parts and hung them too. He traded fruits and vegetables that he grew in exchange for more dolls to hang on the island.

Some may believe that Santana was just a crazy, old man. And he may have been a little off, but I think he believed that he was responsible for protecting the island—and the spirit of the little girl—from evil

The island doll 'population' is around 1,500 according to some accounts while others claim that "many thousands of old dolls and doll parts" litter the island these days.

At one time, Barrera left the island on occasion to get supplies, visit old friends, and such forth. But eventually he became a hermit and never left the island again.

He confessed to his nephew in 2001 that the voices he heard were getting stronger. He felt the end was near for him. His premonition was correct. It wasn't long before his nephew found his uncle floating face down in the same place Barrera had discovered the drowned little girl. The cause of death was a heart attack.

His nephew, Rogelio Sanchez Santana, now owns and protects the island, but he doesn't live on it. But like his uncle, he says he sometimes sees "some shadows in the night with the moonlight". Some visitors have claimed to have witnessed the dolls eyes moving and hearing them talk and locals swear they have seen ghosts and hear shadows talking. They believe the island is cursed.

There is also a well-known story about the Weeping Woman who roams these islands on foggy nights crying out for her lost children.

Island visitors have heard footsteps in the darkness, tormented screams, whispering, giggling, and they claim they feel the dolls' eyes are watching their every move while they on the island.

 **FYI: According to legend, a spirit known as "La Llorona" (Weeping Woman or Crying Woman) roams the area. She is seen crying and seems to be searching for someone. It is believed that she is looking for her children. La Llorona went crazy when her husband left her for another woman. She drowned their children in the river to make her husband suffer, but as soon as she did it, she realized what she'd done. Not able to live with herself, she drowned herself in the same river. Legend has it that if a man sees the Weeping Woman and goes after her to see if he can help, he is never seen again. She is vengeful against all men because of what her husband did to her.**

 Visitors should bring a gift to appease the island's spirits. It should be presented immediately upon arriving on the island. The Island of Dolls is a two-hour boat ride from Mexico City. There is a small admission fee that helps with island upkeep.

http://www.isladelasmunecas.com/Visit-Island-of-the-Dolls-Mexico.html

HANGING COFFINS OF SAGADA
(Philippines)

It is hard to imagine a creepier sight no creepier sight than a bunch of coffins and death chairs hammered into the side of a mountain.

This is an extraordinary—and dangerous—task. It seems strange and unnecessary, but the Igorot tribe feel it must be done. They believe that burying a body in the ground makes for a long ascension to Heaven, whereas "hanging the coffins" high up on the cliffs makes it an easier and faster ascent.

It also makes sense as far as keeping the coffins safe from nature. High up like this, they are safe from flooding, looting, and animals.

While most of us have some fear of death, the Igorot do not. In fact, they embrace it by carving their own coffins out of hollowed logs and preparing the body for the afterlife.

The corpse is "smoked" to help preserve it. The deceased is then settled into a wooden sangadil (death chair) and covered with a blanket and secured with ties. The chair is placed facing the main door of the house so that relatives can pay their respects. A vigil is held for several days and then the body is removed from the death chair and carried to its coffin.

It is considered good luck to have contact with the dead, so mourners usually touch the corpse or at least the blanket it is wrapped in. Traditionally, they are buried in the fetal position because the Igorots believe a person should depart this world the same way he or she entered it.

Upon reaching the burial site, young men climb up the side of the steep cliff where the coffin has been nailed. Sometimes, the death chair is also hanged near the coffin.

The coffins are bigger these days because relatives don't want to break bones to force the body into fetal position. That is a 2,000-year-old tradition that is no longer honored by most. In fact, hanging coffins are a dying tradition (no pun intended). Younger relatives prefer to visit their loved ones in graveyards. The last cliff burial was in 2010.

If you go, do not attempt to climb up the cliff or touch the coffins. You can drive on your own or hire a guide. Buses run from Cubao to Sagada. It is a long journey and should not be attempted during the rainy season.

FYI: Locals called it Echo Valley because when there was a burial here, the village elders would shout and the noise would echo around the valley and they believed they could communicate with the dead.

FYI: Hanging coffins are also a tradition in parts of China and Indonesia.

DEATH ISLAND (Italy)

"Black Death" is a pandemic that first ravaged
Europe from 1347 – 1351. It killed more people
than any other known epidemic or war up to that
time. The Bubonic Plague is spread mostly by
fleas on rodents and other animals. Humans who
are bitten by infected fleas come down with the
plague. It's an example of a disease that can
spread between animals and people.

To stop the deadly spread, there were

quarantine stations. One was located on Death Island, which is officially known as Poveglia Island. It is believed that 150,000 – 190,000 people died a "Black Death" on this little island. They were burned and buried in mass graves, which have since been discovered. Tragically, one in every three Europeans succumbed to the Bubonic Plague.

In the 17th century, the Venetian government built five octagonal forts to protect the harbor, including a fort on Poveglia. Although all buildings are in a sad state of disrepair, the church, hospital, asylum, administrative buildings, living quarters, and bell tower still exist. The bell tower was once used as a lighthouse.

During its time as a quarantine station, everyone coming into Venice had to go through this checkpoint and be cleared before they could proceed. People were held on Poveglia for forty days to make sure they weren't infected. Folks who were suspected of having the plague were dragged out of their homes and brought to Poveglia.

If they didn't have it prior to arriving on the island, they certainly had it after being confined on a tiny, infected island for forty days. The plague pits, where many were "buried" in mass graves, can still be seen today.

In addition to housing a fort and quarantine station, the island has also housed an asylum, nursing home, and prison.

In 1922, Poveglia transformed into an asylum for the mentally ill and a long-term care facility for the elderly. The asylum closed in 1968 and the nursing home shut down in 1975.

Attempts were made to turn the island into an agricultural resource, but that idea was soon abandoned. This is probably due to the soil being unusable. The first thing visitors notice is the stench of Sulphur and death. Next, they notice the sticky ash that covers the island that's a result of the plague bodies being burned. Even after death there was a risk of getting the plague so bodies were burned. In fact, some claim Poveglia is comprised of fifty percent dirt and fifty percent ashes.

Locals refuse to go to the island and fishermen won't go near it because skeletal remains get caught in their nets. Erosion and poor burial methods have "freed" some corpses so that bones are found in the waters around the island. As if that wasn't reason enough, the fishermen have also heard screams and cries coming from the deserted island.

But these restless spirits haven't just been heard, some have been seen. One of the most often seen is "Little Maria," the spirit of a young child who presumably died here from the Plague. She is seen crying and roaming the beach. Pietro, a man with two amputated legs, reportedly raced his wheelchair through the hospital. People claim they can still hear his phantom wheelchair racing up and down the old corridors. The spirit of a young female has also been seen. She has a terrifying expression on her face.

Poveglia is commonly known as "Death Island" and also as "Plague Island."

There were three waves of bubonic plague. The island served as a quarantine station for two of those outbreaks. Sadly, most who came to the island never left it because the odds of surviving the plague before antibiotics were invented was slim to none.

Plague victims weren't just buried here

upon their deaths. According to rumors, the sick were helped on their way. To expedite the inevitable and make room for more victims, those hovering between life and death were burned alive and then discarded into the plague pits. There were no proper burials. These were mass graves containing thousands of corpses. No wonder this is considered to be one of the most haunted places in all of Italy. *So creepy!*

A ghostly fog sometimes appears that seems to swallow the island. It is believed that the island is haunted by the angry spirits of those who died here. Many visitors over the years claim to have been pushed, kicked, shoved, choked, and struck by unseen spirits.

And then there are the noises. Screams, moans, coughs, and cries have been heard by many witnesses.

There was no one standing here when this image was taken, so who is this figure clearly seen in the picture?

So much death and suffering makes it easy to see why spirits may be restless. But there is more to this sad story. During the time that there was an asylum on the island, there was cruelty beyond belief. The psychiatric hospital was not a place for healing. It was a place of exile and despair. The patients were mistreated or ignored, at best.

In the 1930s, the chief doctor began conducting horrible experiments on his mental patients. Dubbed "Doctor Death", he performed lobotomies using hammers, chisels, and drills. What he did to those men and women was despicable and inhumane. But in a strange twist, the doctor himself went mad. He claimed to hear voices and see ghosts. A nurse watched him throw himself off the bell tower one night. As he neared the ground, an eerie reddish mist appeared and enveloped him. When it finally disappeared, so had the doctor!

Another version of this story is that the doctor survived the fall, but that this mysterious mist suffocated the doctor, causing his death. That is why the 12th century bell tower is considered to be the most haunted area on the island. Locals claim to hear the bell on occasion even though it is no longer functional.

Asylum patients claimed to have seen shadowy figures resembling ghosts and hearing screaming and anguished wailing that did not sound human. It has been speculated that these are the screams and cries of people being burned to death in the plague pits. But, of course, these claims were dismissed as the usual crazy rants by mental patients.

After sitting empty for years, a family decided to buy the island and build their dream vacation home. That didn't work out so well for them. Their first night on Poveglia something terrible must have happened that changed all their big plans. The daughter was taken to the hospital the first thing the next morning. She had a huge gash on her face that required fourteen stitches. The family never spoke about what happened that night and none of them ever returned to Poveglia.

Developers have tried many times over the years to resurrect the island, but have always failed miserably. In one case, a construction crew was awarded the job to restore the former hospital building. Soon after they began working, the contractors suddenly stopped and fled the island without any explanation. They never returned.

The Italian government has put the island up for auction to raise money to pay down government debt. Italian businessman, Luigi Brugnaro, won the bid. He got a 99-year lease on the island. It is unknown what Brugnaro plans to do with the island, but whatever it is will be a very expensive proposition given the state of the island's buildings. Also, many believe the evil that lurks here will prevent any successful development, at least it has so far.

The island is actually divided by a canal. The only way to get to the island is by private boat or if you can find a local fisherman or boat captain willing to do it. However, the Italian government considers it trespassing to go onto the island without written permission, which can take a long time to get—if at all. Be advised that if you do go, the buildings are in bad shape and are dangerous to explore. There is also the risk of being caught by the government and charged with trespassing. There's also the risk of being attacked by angry spirits…

The old asylum…too creepy!

 **FYI: According to legend, Napoleon once used the island to store weapons. Some small battles took place here from those who discovered its location and tried to steal the weapons. A few died during these skirmishes.**

This aerial view shows just how close the island is to Venice—less than a half a mile. Even so, locals refuse to go there and it still hasn't been developed in all these years since it was abandoned.

KRYŽIŲ KALNAS (Lithuania)

Just outside the city of Siauliai, in northern Lithuania, there is a hill full of thousands of crosses and religious symbols of all sizes and shapes, including pictures of Saints, rosaries, and crucifixes. This hill was once the site of a fort.

The Kryžių Kalnas (Hill of Crosses) originated after an 1831 Russian rebellion, led by Lithuanians and Poles, left hundreds of people dead. There was another unsuccessful rebellion in 1863. Those who died during these revolts were never given proper burials. Families were forbidden by the tsar from proper burials, so this Hill of Crosses is meant as a remembrance.

Normally, such things are comforting, but in this case they are creepy or at least I think so. For one thing, there are 100,000 – 300,000 items (an accurate count is impossible) crammed haphazardly into one small area, so it is a rather overwhelming and somewhat disturbing sight.

And let's not forget that crucifixes were torture devices. Individuals were nailed to them or bound by their hands and feet, then left to be pecked at by birds, abused by locals, and suffer the ravages of exposure for days without perishing. Jesus is the most famous example of this, but this was a popular medieval torture treatment.

It's also creepy and tragic to see all the photos of those who died defending their freedom and way of life who didn't even get honored with a proper burial.

While this is a place of remembrance by

loved ones, it is also a sad reminder of human sacrifice and repression.

During the Soviet era, religion remained banned. Soviet policy toward religion was based on the ideology of Marxism-Leninism, which made atheism the official doctrine of the Communist Party.

That's why in April 1961, the site was bulldozed and burned down by Russian authorities. Even though the Hill of Crosses was destroyed four more times, locals risked serious consequences by rebuilding the site again and again. They did it during the night when there was less risk of being caught.

I'm told that no one has jurisdiction of the Hill of Crosses anymore. It is maintained by volunteers and various non-profit organizations.

FYI: There is no fee to visit and no set visiting hours so you may come at any time but it best to come during daylight hours. The nearest town is Šialiai. There is parking, a small visitor center, souvenir shop, and restrooms on site.

Torture Rack

TORTURE MUSEUM (The Netherlands)

At one time, torturing someone to death was a common practice in many parts of the world. Criminals and those who were persecuted for their religious beliefs were often hanged in the town's gallows or the guillotine.

The "rack" and inquisition chair were used to extort a confession from someone believed to be guilty of a crime or "sin" of believing in an opposing religion or suspected of practicing witchcraft.

The Torture Museum highlights the tools and techniques used from medieval times through the Middle Ages. Visitors will see dozens of objects and instruments used to instill pain and punishment. The names will give you a clue as to the pain and punishment level: Head Crusher, The Rack, The Sling, Thumb Screws, The Saw, Judas Cradle, and The Garotte.

What is downright creepy is not just seeing these inhumane instruments and discovering how they were used to maximize pain and torture, but also to realize that thousands or possibly millions were subjected to these punishments, interrogations, and executions throughout Europe during the Middle Ages.

There is a warning posted in the museum that this is not a place for the faint of heart. This is a gruesome and creepy place that is a brutal reminder of one of the darkest times in history. This is a small museum and does not take long to explore. http://www.torturemuseum.com/

The Inquisition Chair had sharp points from the neck to the ankles that would go in deep enough to break the skin and be very painful, but not enough kill you. Go to https://www.medievalchronicles.com/medieval-torture-devices/ to learn more about medieval torture devices.

FYI: A second similar museum in Amsterdam is the Museum of Medieval Torture Instruments, which is close to the central station. The two museums are not connected.

MUSEUM OF VAMPIRES & LEGENDARY CREATURES (France)

From the moment you enter the Le Musée des Vampires, you realize this is a unique and creepy place. It was founded by eccentric scholar and self-proclaimed vampirologist, Jacques Sirgent. The museum shares the dark history of Paris, including vampire rituals, vintage movie posters, autographed photos of actors who starred in vampire and creature movies, cannibal sorcery, and lots more 'Undead' stuff. You will see a 19th century vampire killing kit, bizarre artwork, rare reference books, Dracula collectibles, and more weird things than you can believe would fit into this small space.

Sirgent simultaneously scares and mesmerizes visitors with his macabre museum. He is a gifted storyteller and has a lifetime of research, so he knows his topic well. Tours are given gladly, but by appointment only.

It is one of the best kept secrets in Paris but you'll know you've arrived at the right place when you see a mock cemetery full of fake bats and real human remains. Just past this cemetery is the museum entrance.
https://www.facebook.com/museedesvampires

This abandoned amusement park was scheduled to open one day after the nuclear disaster occurred.

PRIPYAT (Ukraine)

The Chernobyl Nuclear Power Plant disaster caused a city-wide leak of deadly nuclear radiation. Once home to thousands of plant workers and their families, the city of Pripyat was completely evacuated within three hours. Residents had to flee, leaving behind almost everything.

The Chernobyl disaster was a nuclear accident that occurred on April 26, 1986 at the

No. 4 reactor in the Chernobyl Nuclear Power Plant, near the city of Pripyat in the north of the Ukrainian SSR in the Soviet Union. There was a massive explosion that caused a huge fire that released large amounts of radioactive chemicals in the air. Nearly three dozen people were killed during the explosion. Many more ultimately succumbed to cancer linked to radiation exposure. It is considered the worst nuclear disaster in history both in cost and casualties.

Named after the nearby Pripyat River, Pripyat is in northern Ukraine, which was part of the Soviet Union at that time. It was built to house the employees of the Chernobyl Nuclear Power Plant and became the ninth nuclear city in the Soviet Union.

Pripyat is part of the Chernobyl Exclusion Zone. After the leak, more than 50,000 area inhabitants were quickly bussed out of Pripyat and never permitted to return. The radiation levels remain dangerously high to this day. Even in the exclusion zone, radiation is ten times the normal level. Nothing can be grown here because plants absorb the radiation like a sponge.

In the center of the exclusion area, sits the abandoned reactor and the control room. Mike Durst is a nuclear physicist who is one of the few permitted in this area has described it like "being in a tomb. Cold, wet and dark." He describes burst pipes, lots of debris, and a series of mazes you have to navigate to reach the control room. He says the level of radiation is not too high here, but if you go down below it will kill you.

The authorities allow evacuees to return briefly once a year to visit the graves and honor the memory of their relatives and ancestors during a "Day of the Parents." Families mourn the loss of family members and a way of life that has been lost forever.

At the time of evacuation, there were several schools, a large hospital complex, dozens of shops, gyms, parks, movie theaters, factories, and an amusement park that was scheduled to open the day after the nuclear disaster. It was a lovely place to live. Sadly, Pripyat has been a ghost town ever since the emergency evacuation.

Ever since the accident, the exclusion zone has remained uninhabited except for 500 or so elderly people the *"samosjoly"* who came back, preferring to stay in their homes despite the risks. Also, the military, police, and scientists enter the area as necessary. There is electricity in part of Pripyat. However, it will 20,000 years before Pripyat will be safely habitable again. www.chernobylwel.com

Pripyat is being swallowed up by trees.

 **FYI: Chernobyl and Pripyat tours are given to those interested in visiting the Exclusion Zone. Visitors need a pass issued by the government. Local tour companies based in Kyiv (Hamalia, SoloEast, and SAM Travel Company) can obtain these passes and take you to this area. All tours include lunch with food from outside the contamination zone. Lupine Travel offers overnight stays in Chernobyl for those crazy enough to want one. Due to the lack of maintenance on abandoned buildings, you cannot enter any of the buildings for safety reasons. Tours end with radiation screenings. There is even a visitor's center with a model of the reactor. Pripyat is being consumed by the surrounding forest so it will be off limits soon and eventually gone forever as if it never existed.**

THE GHOST CHURCH (Czech Republic)

In Lukova, Czech Republic, there is a church that was built hundreds of years ago. St. George's Church was consecrated way back in 1352. Most of the townspeople attended services here until the roof fell in during a funeral service. For some reason, locals decided it was because the church was haunted, not because the roof was old.

So, instead of making the necessary repairs and resuming services, the congregation began holding services outside. No one would go inside the "haunted" church anymore, so it has been abandoned since 1968.

In 2012, the volunteer caretaker, Per Koukl, decided to start a fund-raising campaign to repair the roof. He asked local artist and art student, Jakub Hadrava, for help.

Hadrava came up with a very unique idea. He created plaster models of real people and then covered them completely with sheets and shrouds. It is a shocking thing when you first see these thirty-two ghost sculptures sitting in pews and standing in doorways.

Enough money was raised from admission fees to get the roof repaired last year. The church even has concerts and mass on occasion. No one seems concerned anymore about the church being haunted now that it is full of ghost people!

The church is now known as "the ghost church" and is open to the public on Saturdays from 1pm to 4pm, May to October. Roughly 150 visitors come every weekend to see the creepy art installation.

Nowadays, the village of Luková, Jiří, is mostly uninhabited, unless you count the ghostly congregation of the ghost church. Lukova is a tiny town that is 2.5 hours outside of Prague. There is a train that runs from Prague to Lukova. https://lukova-kostel.cz/

More Creepy, Spooky or Just Plain Weird Things to Do in Prague

Museum of Alchemists & Magicians of Old Prague

Magical Cavern

Strahov Monastery

Sex Machines Museum

Nuclear Bunker Museum

Black Light Theatre

Museum of Historical Chamber Pots & Toilets

Ghost Walk

VEIJO RÖNKKÖNEN (Finland)

Art is often subjective and controversial, but this is just plain creepy! Veijo Rönkkönen Sculpture Park is named after the Finnish artist who created its 550 concrete sculptures.

Two hundred of these sculptures are nude and posing in various yoga positions. If you are familiar with yoga, you know there are some strange positions, such as Upward Dog, Reclining Hero's Pose, and Handstand Scorpion.

While these sculptures are just a little bit creepy, the other sculptures he created, such as a cloaked man with outstretched arms that seem to be reaching out to grab you and a scary-looking nun hiding behind some bushes. Are totally creepy.

These sculptures are freakishly realistic as far as facial features, especially the eyes and teeth (many have human teeth and black, sunken eyes). Many visitors have sworn that these sinister-looking sculptures seem to be staring right at them, as if they are about to come to life. And there are non-human figures, as well. These are odd treelike sculptures with cone-shaped branches.

Rönkkönen was a notoriously reclusive and eccentric artist before his death in 2010. The artist spent fifty years creating this unique sculpture garden.

These creepy creatures in the Veijo Rönkkönen Sculpture Garden in Parikkala, Finland draw thousands of visitors annually. http://www.patsaspuisto.net/#english

CITY OF GHOSTS (China)

Fengdu Ghost City is a collection of shrines, statues, and monuments dedicated to death and the afterlife. So that is a tad bit creepy, but it gets worse.

According to Chinese legend, Fengdu is where the Devil lives. Godly spirits go to Heaven, but evil spirits go to Fengdu. This is reportedly the home of Tianzi, the King of the Dead. A temple is located on Ming Shan Hill that is dedicated to Tianzi.

The city is underwater and Ming Shan

Hill is now an island full of Taoist tombs and graves, as well as temples and shrines.

The huge face on the hill is "The Ghost King". It holds a Guinness Book of World Records title as the biggest rock sculpture.

Fengdu has been in existence for roughly 2,000 years. Its origins date back to the Han Dynasty (206 BCE – 220 CE) when two officials, Yin and Wang, decided to run away to this place to live out the rest of their days. According to legend, they became immortal.

Most of the sites in Fengdu are a reference to the afterlife, such as Ghost Torturing Pass and Last Glance to Home Tower.

More recent additions include a haunted house depicting terrors of the afterlife and a cable car that takes visitors up to the temple of Tianzi or you can climb the path, which takes about fifteen to twenty minutes. You can't get lost. Just look for the temple with statues of three-toed demons eating people, blue demons, and people suffering in hell. You'll also see vendors selling all kinds of scary stuff, such as the masks worn by the killer in the *Scream* movie franchise, which may be the most disturbing thing you'll see here.

Fengdu is 100 miles east of Chongqing in the Three Gorges Lake, at the northern end of the Yangtze River. It attracts tourists from all over China and the world. Yangtze River Cruises go right by it. The site is divided into two parts—heaven and hell. Separate tickets are required for each one.

HOIA BACIU FOREST (Romania)

Hoia Baciu Forest is more commonly known as "The Bermuda Triangle of Transylvania." There are many rumors as to who or what is here. Some say it's the angry spirits of murdered villagers. Others have claimed to have seen UFOs and aliens while in these woods.

This forest first became famous in the 1960s. Biologist Alexandru Sift was here conducting tests when he saw a flying object just above the trees. He got a photograph of it and there is no doubt it is not an airplane, at least not like any we've seen. That makes it an unidentified flying object or UFO.

A shepherd and his large flock of sheep

simply vanished in this area never to be seen again. A five-year-old girl disappeared and reappeared five years later. She had not aged one day and was wearing the same clothes. She has no memory of what happened during the time she was missing. A popular theory was an alien abduction. There are many more stories of mysterious disappearances here.

After leaving the forest, hikers have discovered scratches, rashes, and burns on their bodies that were not there before they went into the forest. They cannot explain where or how they got them. The feeling of nausea and headaches is also common. Higher than normal radioactivity has been discovered here.

A lot of paranormal activity is consistently reported in one area of the forest. No vegetation grows in this area called "The Clearing" and it is in the shape of a circle. The soil has been tested and no scientific reason has been discovered as to why nothing grows in this one place.

The Clearing

In 1968, military technician, Emil Barnea, was visiting the forest one August afternoon along with his girlfriend and two friends. His girlfriend shouted and pointed to the sky. Barnea and the others ran over to where she was standing and looked up to see what looked like a silver disk hovering over "The Clearing". He took a few photos before it disappeared from view about two minutes later.

Some believe it is an alien landing site and that is why nothing will grow there. Barnea lost his government job after local newspapers published his photos and interview. An investigation proved that no commercial flights or weather balloons were in this area at that time.

Many visitors have emerged from these woods with photos of strange phenomena, such as unexplainable lights, ectoplasms, and mysterious spheres appearing in the forest. Shadow figures and ghostly apparitions have been seen. The woods are thought to be haunted by Romanian peasants who were murdered here.

This 616-acre forested area is considered to be one of the creepiest and most haunted places in Romania because there is so much documentation of paranormal activity (or at least activity that defies logical explanation). While scientists from around the world are still taking soil samples, studying the twisted trees, and searching for rational explanations, some speculate the forest is a portal to another world or parallel universe.

The Hoia Baciu Forest is about a twenty-minute drive from Cluj Napoca, which is on the northern border of Romania. Day and night tours are offered by local guides or you can explore on your own—if you dare. There are hiking and biking paths and lots of wildlife to be seen.

The forest is full of these strange-looking trees. Many trees here grow in spiral or zig-zag patterns and always in a clockwise direction, a phenomenon that scientists cannot explain despite much research and investigation.

THE DOLL VILLAGE (Japan)

The village of Nagaro is in the Iya Valley surrounded by picturesque mountains. It is a lovely place to live. Unfortunately, to get to the nearest hospital, grocery store, or job prospect, residents have to drive at least ninety minutes along narrow, winding roads.

Nagoro's story isn't different from that of many other small towns and villages around the world. As older folks pass away and young people move to the city to find jobs, the result is a shrinking population that often causes the town or village to fade away.

At one time, Nagaro had a medical clinic

and several businesses, including a pachinko gambling parlor, inn, general store, and a diner. Now, it doesn't even have one shop. The village school closed in 2012.

A resident, Tsukimi Ayano, who moved away and came home several years later was shocked and displeased with what she found. She decided to do something about it. If human inhabitants couldn't be found, she'd create her own village population.

Ayano began making life-size dolls to help populate Nagaro. She has spent ten years on this project so far. During this time, she has made more than 350 dolls.

Now here's where it gets creepy. The doll

maker didn't just make dolls. She made life-size dolls that resembled people who once lived here. She started with her own family and carried on with neighbors, teachers, and so on. Supposedly, Ayano has made a perfect replica of her mother to keep her company at home and created one of her grandmother who rides with her when she needs to go to the next town to go shopping.

The dolls are made of wire and stuffed with straw and newspaper. They are dressed in clothes their human counterparts would have worn. The clothing has been donated from folks all over the country as word spread about what Ayano's project.

The dolls have been strategically placed all over the village. They are sitting in classrooms. They are working in gardens. They are sitting on porches. They are fishing in the river. They are standing along the road. They are working in the fields.

Some of these dolls are rather strange, such as the six boy dolls wearing potato sacks and standing beside a bridal party on the school's stage.

During the 1950s and '60s, the area was buzzing with forestry projects, road construction and dam building for hydroelectric plants. But once the dams were built, many people left. In its heyday, the village had a population of around 350.

Today, that population is less than 30 and most of the villagers are elderly. Soon, the village will probably become extinct except for its doll inhabitants.

FYI: Japan's Hashima Island is more commonly known as Ghost Island. The population peak was in 1959 with 5,259 residents. By 1974, the coal reserves were depleted, the mine closed, and the people left. The island has long been abandoned, except for tourists who come to see the ghost town. An occasional movie has been filmed here, including the James Bond flick, *Skyfall*. Ghost Island is reportedly haunted by the spirits of Chinese and Korean laborers who were tortured and died here during WWII. Government sanctioned tours are permitted, but you cannot visit on your own. www.gunkanjima-concierge.com

BLOOD FALLS (Antarctica)

This remarkable phenomenon is a five-story, blood red waterfall. Taylor Glacier (aka "Blood Falls") began forming five million years when the glacier sealed off a lake beneath it.

Devoid of light and oxygen but rich in microbes, the water became more and more concentrated with salt and iron content. The salt prevents the water from freezing and the iron gives it this unique crimson color when it comes into contact with the air. It escapes through a fissure in the glacier.

It is a bit creepy to see what looks like blood endlessly flowing out of a glacier. It looks like it could be a crime scene.

Blood Falls is only accessible by helicopter from the U.S. research station, McMurdo Station, New Zealand's Scott Base, or a cruise ship sailing in the Ross Sea.

U.S. Research Station, McMurdo Base, in Antarctica

More weird waterfalls…

Fog Waterfall (Iceland): This waterfall does not appear all the time; several conditions must accompany this – firstly, the direction of the wind, and secondly, a specific air temperature. The anomaly, the researchers believe, was caused by temperature inversion – an increase in air temperature with altitude.

Horizontal Flow Waterfalls (Australia):
Horizontal Falls are two natural phenomena
found in Talbot Bay in Western
Australia. Polton Creek, two elongated
freshwater bodies of water, separate the small
McLarty ridges from Talbot Bay. And in these
mountain ranges, there are two gorges. Water
accumulates in front of the gorges faster than
flowing through them. It creates a difference in
water levels in the bay and Polton Creek and
creates the effect of a waterfall. However, unlike
classical waterfalls, this natural phenomenon
runs horizontally, creating the illusion that water
spreads over the bay's surface.

Cameron Falls (Canada): Cameron Falls is
near Ruby Ridge in Waterton Lakes National
Park. This is home to red rocks with oxidized
iron called clayey siltstones. After a heavy rain,
the waterfall sometimes turns a bubble gum pink
color. The best chance of seeing this is in May
or June when heavy rains are most likely

Mauritius Underwater Waterfall (Mauritius):
The illusion of an underwater waterfall in
Mauritius arises from solid underwater
currents. These solid underwater currents, which
constantly erode the sand, contributed to
forming a high plateau that appeared in the
ocean. The relief of the seabed, formed by coral
reefs, sand, and silt, moves under the influence
of powerful underwater currents and creates a
similar optical illusion in the form of an
underwater waterfall. The crystal clear water
within the coral reef further enhances this unique
illusion. The simplest way to get to the
underwater waterfall of Mauritius is by
helicopter sightseeing tours. Air Mauritius
organizes these helicopter tours in Mauritius.

Pamukkale Waterfall (Turkey)
Nature created these thermal springs. The water
has a very high salt content and over time a
cascade of snow-white formations has formed,
resembling a frozen waterfall. Pamukkale is also
called Cleopatra's pool. According to legend, it
was here that the Egyptian queen drew her

beauty and youth. It is best to visit it in October, November, April, and May.

Pamukkale Waterfall

CENTRALIA (Pennsylvania, USA)

Centralia was a nice little town that was growing and prospering, thanks to its profitable coal mines. But all that changed when a mine caught fire in 1962. Ironically, it started with a controlled fire at the town landfill.

The fire department lined the pit with an incombustible material to contain the fire, which they lit on the night of May 27, 1962. After the landfill's contents were ash, they doused the remaining embers with water.

But two days later, residents reported seeing flames. Centralia firefighters used bulldozers to remove the burned garbage and made a horrible discovery.

At the bottom of the trash pit was a large hole about 15-feet wide and several feet deep. Garbage had previously concealed this hole, which meant it had not been filled with fire-retardant material. The result was that this hole provided a path directly to the labyrinth of old coal mines over which the town was built.

Residents began complaining of foul odors in the air and smoke coming out of the ground around the landfill. The town council brought in a mine inspector to check the smoke, who determined that the levels of carbon monoxide were unacceptable and all area mines were immediately shut down.

Despite repeated efforts, officials were never able to put out the subterranean fire. Scientists say it will burn another 250 years at least.

Although the citizens of Centralia were

aware of the subterranean fire, they weren't too concerned until a little boy fell into a sinkhole in his backyard and the deadly carbon monoxide began seeping into homes and businesses. Also, trees began to die, the ground turned to ash, and roads and sidewalks began to buckle. And some folks developed a bad cough from the smoke.

Congress approved millions of dollars in relocation money and most people took the money and left town. Even though Centralia is commonly referred to as a ghost town, it still has inhabitants. It seems a toxic fire is not enough to make everybody want to leave. Some folks were determined to stay and they fought the government to do so. For the next decade, a group of residents battled it out in court.

In 2013, the remaining dozen or so residents won a cash settlement and ownership of their properties until they die. At that time, the state of Pennsylvania will seize the land and demolish all remaining structures, as it has already done with those all the other homes.

By 2017, only six residents remained. When they go, Centralia will truly be a ghost town. Visitors will probably not be permitted once the government takes over the town completely. If you visit, be aware that the ground does collapse underneath people sometimes. Residents say you get used to it!

Ironically, the town is growing all the while the government is trying to erase it. The 2022 census revealed a population of 14, which means the population has more than doubled over the last five years. https://worldpopulationreview.com/us-cities/centralia-pa-population

The lovely Assumption of the Blessed Virgin Mary Ukrainian Greek-Catholic Church still sits on a hill above town and continues to hold weekly services. The town once had six churches but now this is the only church still standing.

FYI: The last few holdouts have to have post office boxes in another town or have their mail sent somewhere else because the postal code has been removed. The town is no longer called Centralia. By order of the government, it has been removed from all buildings and signs. This means that residents have trouble getting deliveries or any type of service. The county records office has begun the process of erasing Centralia from its records. Due to all the underground damage, the remaining homes need additional supports, so visitors will see several chimneys built up the exterior  **of the houses. Visitors are permitted but be aware they are not welcomed by residents because they tend to leave behind trash and graffiti.**

GOMANTONG CAVES (Malaysia)

There are two cave complexes – Simud Hitam (Black Cave) and Simud Putih (White Cave). The caves have limestone walls that are up to 300 feet tall.

This place is the perfect location for a

horror movie because Gomantong has roughly two million bats hanging off the walls and ceilings (I don't know who or how they counted the bats). So I think we're all in agreement that a cave full of millions of bats is pretty creepy. But then there's the guano (bat poop) that is *everywhere*. Okay, so maybe that's more gross than creepy. But the several million Malaysian cockroaches that are running all over the place are downright creepy. Why so many? It's because they love bat poop. Wherever there is guano, there are cockroaches galore.

But that's not all. There are many more creepy creatures found in these caves, such as snakes, rats, scorpions, cave crabs, and giant scutigera centipedes, which are three-inches-long, and poisonous. There's also the wrinkle-lipped, free-tailed bats (let's just call them bats) who usually sleep during the day, unless you disturb them.

But there are thousands of black birds (swiftlets) that fly around the caves during the day. Yes, they also poop. *Everywhere*. Their nests hang on the walls of the caves, and these nests are edible (so they say). In fact, they're used in parts of Asia for bird's nest soup, so they're considered to be very valuable. You may see guards in the cave, but they're not there to protect you. They're paid to protect those edible bird nests.

But the cockroaches and dung beetles are more worrisome than the bats or birds. You will step on them since they are crawling everywhere. It simply cannot be avoided. So you need to wear high boots in the caves. You will want them anyway because of the snakes and rats. You should also bring a mask because the smell from all the poop is overwhelming and unhealthy to breathe.

There is even a sign posted at the entrance of the cave warning visitors about "wild animals." Orangutans, raptors, and other not-so-friendly animals hang around the caves so you have to watch out for them. Guides will warn visitors to keep quiet during the short trek to the mouth of the cave to avoid encountering these wild animals. You should also be advised to wear lots of insect repellent and a hat on your head (don't ask why, just do it!)

The bats exit the caves at dusk nightly if you'd like to see them take flight. The easiest way to get to the Gomantong Caves is to join half-day tours departing from Sandakan town.

Cockroaches and giant, poisonous centipedes are just a few of the creepy inside the cave.

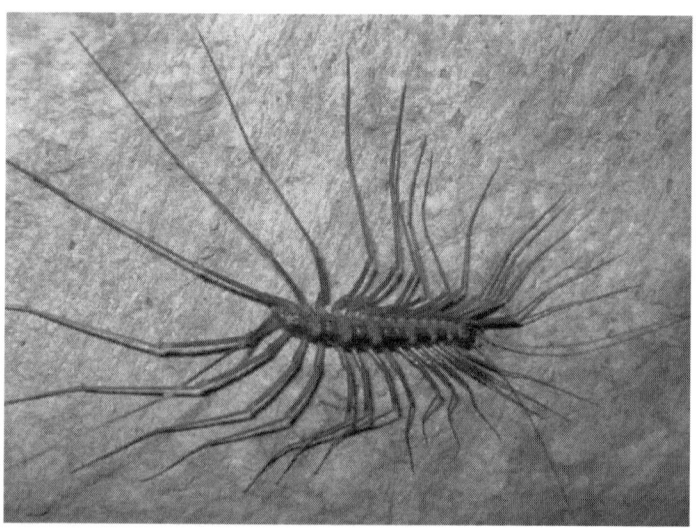

Gomantong Caves

Gomantong Caves is a limestone cave system consisting of nine caves, with the two largest caves being *Simud Putih* (White Cave) and *Simud Hitam* (Black Cave). The caves were discovered in 1930.

Creepy...check!

Stinky...absolutely!

Deadly...possibly!

Disgusting...definitely!

CAPUCHIN CATACOMBS (Italy)

Catacombe dei Cappucini (Capuchin Catacombs) was created back in the late 16th century when the cemetery at the Capuchin monastery was full beyond capacity. Men of the cloth were originally intended to be the only ones entombed here, but once word got out about the mummification processes taking place in the catacombs, it soon became *the* place for eternal slumber.

Prominent citizens made sure to score a spot in these sacred catacombs. They even left instructions about what they wanted to wear, which was their best attire.

So these underground tombs were divided into separate burial corridors: one for clergy, one for men, and one for women, children, and virgins.

"Sleeping Beauty"

The oldest corpse is a friar, Silvestro da Gubbio, who passed away in 1599. The youngest corpse is Rosalia Lombardo. In 1920, she died of pneumonia when she was just two years old. She is laid out in a glass casket wearing her best party dress. She has been dubbed "Sleeping Beauty" because she has been so well preserved it looks like she is sleeping.

Visitors are permitted in the catacombs. But you should be prepared for a creepy sight. There are well-dressed corpses everywhere displayed in all kinds of positions, such as sitting, standing, and laying in open coffins. Many have sunken cheeks and mouths hanging open due to decomposing facial ligaments and gravity. The lights are dim and the catacombs are musty. It seems like the perfect backdrop for a horror movie, such as *The Mummy*.

The monks embalming process was lengthy and involved a drying room with a ceramic pipe draining system. The embalming formula included zinc salts (to give the body rigidity), glycerin (to prevent body from over drying), salicylic acid (to kill fungi), alcohol (to dry the body out), and formalin (to kill bacteria). Once the corpses had completed the embalming process, a vinegar solution was used to "bathe" them. The bodies were stuffed with hay and dressed in their Sunday best. Some wealthy families even provided costume changes! Priests were dressed in clerical vestments and military men wore their dress uniforms for eternity.

The website provides directions on how to get to the catacombs, as well as hours of operation and costs.
http://www.palermocatacombs.com/

The most disturbing mummies are the children.

CEMETERY CITY (Guatemala)

You won't find traditional cemeteries here. Due to a high death rate and a shortage of space, Guatemala City builds vertical cemeteries known as the "City of the Dead". Coffins are stacked one on top of another, row after row. Ladders are used to access the higher crypts.

As if this isn't a creepy enough sight, the local hang out is along the alleys, in front of the coffins.

Here you will find vendors selling everything from cold drinks to coffin cushions. Local bands play mourning music. Friends and family of the deceased dance in front of the stacks of coffins and socialize with one another.

Rent must be paid if the deceased are to be allowed to rest in peace. The first six years are free, but after that a fee is charged every four years. There is a high poverty rate here so many cannot afford these fees.

In those cases, the bodies are removed, wrapped in clear plastic bags, and left in the street. Relatives must come claim them quickly. If not, they are buried in mass, unmarked graves. If you are there early in the morning, you will witness the bodies being pulled out of the coffins as they do it right out in the open.

Sadly, this happens every morning. You always know exactly when this happens because vultures can be seen flying over the cemetery city when the coffins are broken open. If you plan to visit, be prepared for the foul stench of death in the air. But even more disturbing is the pile of corpses you will see if you visit during the morning hours.

La Verbena Cemetery is in Guatemala City.

HAW PAR VILLA (Singapore)

Haw Par Villa is an old theme park that is unlike any theme park you've ever visited. You won't find any Disney kind of rides here or whimsical shows.

What you will find is lots of creepy statues and dioramas of people being tortured, punished, and killed in some cases. They are meant to teach kids about morality and mythology, but more likely they are traumatized by when they see—if they even understand what they are looking at.

Haw Par Villa was built in 1937 and abandoned when WWII broke out. Fifty years later, an attempt was made to reopen the park. But it was decided that it was too expensive to modernize it, so that was the end of that.

However, several years later, the Singapore Tourism Board bought the land and restored the original 1,000 statues and 150 dioramas.

The park's crowning glory is its Ten Courts of Hell, which is now known as Hell's Museum. According to Chinese mythology, after a person dies, they arrive at the First Court of Hell. King Qinguang decides if they are worthy to enter paradise. If not, they are sent to the Mirror of Retribution and then punished. The statues get creepier as you proceed through the courts.

By the Ninth Court of Hell, visitors will see statues without heads and arms because they have been chopped off as punishment for unlawful conduct. The Tenth Court is ruled by Hu Fa Shi, a big, green monster with scary eyes who can control ghosts and devils.

If you want to see this unique theme park, it is free to go and the park is open daily. There is a fee to enter Hell's Museum, which is so dark and disturbing that children are not permitted to enter it. Hell's Museum is closed on Mondays and Tuesdays.
https://www.visitsingapore.com/see-do-singapore/culture-heritage/heritage-discovery/haw-par-villa/

Haw Par Villa is the only theme park of its kind in the world. *Thank goodness!*

One of the park's strangest displays is a giant crab with the head of a boy.

AKODESSAWA FETISH MARKET (West Africa)

This place is absolutely the creepiest thing I've ever seen. It is the world's largest voodoo market. The market is in Lomé, Togo, which is full of voodoo practitioners. This is not surprising given that it is the birthplace of voodoo. Many think it began in Haiti or New Orleans, but it originated in West Africa.

The voodoo practitioners come here to shop for ingredients needed to create their charms and fetishes. There are rows and rows and rows of vendor stalls. Also, there are huts to hold consultations with fetish priests, seers, psychics, and traditional doctors.

Akodessawa is full of things you will not find anywhere else (thankfully), such as crocodile heads, human skulls, chimpanzee hands, horsetails, dead birds, dried snakes, and lots of bones.

There is every kind of animal you can think of for sale in varying degrees of decay.

There are thousands of piles of horns, antlers, teeth, eyes, sex organs, feet, skulls, paws, skins, and bones. These items are typically ground up to make powders and potions to be used in charms, spells, and rituals for everything from better sex to curing ailments.

There are no fixed prices. Sellers will consult with the gods until both parties reach an acceptable price. Additional items needed for charms and rituals can also be found here, such as dolls and clothes.

It may be just another day at the office for voodoo priests, but for the rest of us this is a creepy place likely to cause nightmares! And if the sight of all these things doesn't get you, the smell will do it. You can't even imagine! But if you must see it for yourself, the market is open daily. It is free but there is a fee for taking photos.

Voodoo dolls are sold at the market. A voodoo doll represents a specific person and they are typically used for healing or revenge.

SNAKE ISLAND (Brazil)

The name says it all. This is an island full of snakes. Just snakes. Deadly snakes. Ninety miles off the coast of São Paulo, Ilha de Queimada Grande (Snake Island) is one of the most dangerous islands in the entire world. There are up to five snakes every ten feet, which rates high up on the creepy meter!

Approximately 11,000 years ago, rising

sea levels separated Snake Island from mainland Brazil. This resulted in "super snakes".

Seriously! These isolated snakes became hyper evolved. They had no predators so they quickly multiplied. Without any ground-level prey on the island, the snakes learned to hunt in the treetops and strike at birds from the air. And because they couldn't track down the birds and wait for the poison to kick in, their venom adapted to become five times stronger than that that of regular snakes. *These are the world's most poisonous snakes.*

Their lethal venom can kill prey instantly. Scientists say these snakes can melt human flesh with their poisonous venom. Because they are so deadly, the Brazilian government has banned the public from the island (as if you would want to go).

Do you want to guess how many snakes are here? At one time, the population was estimated to be 430,000 snakes. But recent estimates are closer to 250,000.

There are as many as 4,000 Golden Lancehead Vipers on the island, which is the deadliest snake in the world. They are found mostly in the rainforest area of the island.

Golden Lancehead Snake

There are lots of stories and legends about Snake Island, such as the one about the last lighthouse keeper. From 1909 to the 1920s, there was a functioning lighthouse on the island. A lighthouse keeper and his family lived there until they were found dead with hundreds of snake bites when a cadre of snakes slithered into the

keeper's house through the windows. The
lighthouse is still there but is now automated.

The 5,000-foot-long and 1,600-foot wide island
is an important laboratory for biologists and
researchers, who are granted special permission
to visit the island in order to study its snakes,
especially the Golden Lancehead, which is an
endangered species.

There are also sixty-eight species of birds,
two bat species, two amphibian species, two
amphisbaenid species and three species of
lizards. There are no land mammals on the
island.

Because of black market demand by
scientists and animal collectors, snake
smugglers, sneak onto Ilha da Queimada Grande

on occasion. They trap the snakes and sell them on the black market for enough money to make it worth the risk to them. One Golden Lancehead snake can sell for as much as $30,000—if the smugglers make it off the island alive.

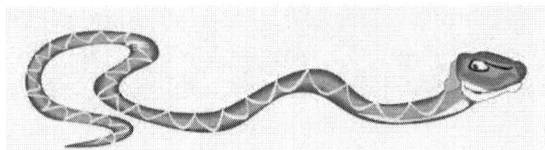

AOKIGAHARA FOREST (Japan)

Not only is Aokigahara the most famous forest in Japan, it is also one of the most well-known worldwide. This place has been dubbed Sea of Trees, Suicide Forest, and Japan's Demon Forest.

Aokigahara Forest extends more than fourteen miles and is so dense that it is always dark and creepy. To the contrary of most wooded places, this is not a habitat for wildlife. Visitors should not expect to see or hear any animals, save an occasional bird. In fact, visitors should expect to hear a chilling silence.

Visitors should also take care as these woods are dangerous due to the rocky terrain and numerous precipices and caves, including the eerily beautiful Ice Cave and Wind Cave. There are more than 200 caves inside the forest.

Between the darkness and vast network of roots and vines, this is a place one can easily get hurt. There are thousands of trees and most of these trees date back more than three hundred years so they are huge, which is why no sunlight can be seen.

Also, it is unnaturally quiet due to the absence of wildlife and its remote location, which means no traffic, music, voices, or any other noise. One can't help but feel disoriented and alone in these strange woods.

Due to the rich deposits of magnetic iron in the volcanic soil, compasses, cell phones, and GPS are useless. You are totally and completely on your own and at great risk of getting lost.

Many visitors to Aokigahara are not worried about getting lost because they never intend to leave. Aokigahara is the second most popular place to commit suicide in the world (Golden Gate Bridge in San Francisco, USA is the #1 suicide spot).

There have been hundreds of suicides here since the 1950s. By the 1970s, the situation had reached crisis level and the government began conducting sweeps of the forest to recover bodies. The numbers continued to increase exponentially over the years. Recently, the Japanese government stopped reporting the deaths in an effort to curtail this tragic activity.

The most active time for suicides is March, which is the end of the fiscal year in Japan. The most common methods are hanging and drug overdose. Thankfully, not all suicides are successful. But for those who achieve their objective, they are often disturbed even in death. Corpse robbers sweep the forest more often than the authorities looking for valuables that may be on the deceased, such as money and jewelry.

Once the bodies are recovered by the proper authorities, they are taken back to town and placed in a special room reserved just for these suicide corpses. A representative from forest services is selected to spend the night in this room with the corpse. The reason for this supervision is because the Japanese believe that if a corpse is left alone, it is bad for the spirit of the deceased.

You may wonder how this place became a suicide hot spot. In 1960, Author Seicho Matsumoto published *Kuroi Kaiju (Black Sea of Trees)*. This is a story about two lovers who commit suicide in Aokigahara Forest. While this may have escalated activity, suicides were recorded well before the book's publication. A more likely culprit would be Wataru Tsurumui's book, *The Complete Suicide Manual*, which is often found beside the deceased in this forest.

While the tortured souls of these suicide victims are believed to haunt these woods, there are plenty more ghosts roaming around.

From ancient times until the 19th century, families practiced a Japanese ritual known as ubasute or obasute. The rough translation is "abandoning a parent." According to legend, families brought elderly family members into the woods and left them to die of starvation, dehydration, or exposure—whichever came first.

This is the Japanese version of euthanasia. It is unclear whether the family did this on their own accord or if this was mandated by feudal officers. This sacrifice of the oldest and weakest was done in the hopes of saving the rest of the family from doom during times of famine and drought. The unhappy spirits of those who suffered these horrible fates are believed to linger here. It is believed that these spirits are vengeful and will cause harm to anyone who wanders these woods, especially the weak and the sad.

More unhappy spirits can be found here, as well. Demonic spirits are believed to float from tree to tree. They appear as weird-looking white shapes before disappearing behind the next tree. They keep vigil over this forest and all those who enter it.

Japanese spiritualists believe these spirits, known as "Yurei" (Ghosts of the Dead), have become part of the trees and seeped into the soil to create a powerfully negative, supernatural energy that preys on those who come here seeking solutions. If there are any doubts when they arrive, being in these sinister, spooky woods does nothing to dispel suicidal thoughts. To the contrary, the intent becomes intense and persistent.

There have been investigations of these haunted woods over the years, including SyFy's *Destination Truth*. The results are always the same. They see shadows they can't identify as human or animal. They hear voices but the woods are devoid of any other humans as far as they can tell. Also, they feel an unfriendly presence around them and begin having dark, confusing thoughts.

Many supernatural, thriller, and horror movies have been filmed here, including *The Forest, The Sea of Trees, Aokigahara, Grave Halloween*, and *The Mourning Forest*.

FYI: The Japanese believe in "onryo", which are angry ghosts who seek revenge on those who wronged them while they were alive. The Japanese believe these vengeful ghosts can cause natural disasters. A well-known "Onryo" is Oiwa. According to legend, she is the spirit of a woman whose husband poisoned her and treated her badly. Oiwa wears a worn white dress and has long, loose hair, although she is partially bald. The baldness and a drooping left eye are believed to be side effects of the poisoning she endured.

The forest is 100 miles west of Tokyo at the base of Mount Fuji. The closest town is Fujikawaguchiko, which is in the Minamitsuru

District. You can take the train (Fujikyuko and Shiojiri lines) to get there.

It is recommended you hire a guide as it is easy to get lost. Compasses, GPS, and cellphones are useless in the forest due to the volume of magnetic iron in the volcanic soil. At the very least, it is recommended that you carry plastic tape to mark your path as you go so that you don't get hopelessly lost.

Coordinates: 35°28′12″N 138°37′11″E

http://aokigaharaforest.com/Aokigahara-getting-there.html

FYI: Fuji-Hakone-Izu National Park is divided into these areas: Mount Fuji, Shiraito Falls, Fuji Five Lakes, Aokigahara, and Lake Tanuki. Cities near the park include Odawara, Fuji, and Numazu.
htttp://www.env.go.jp/en/nature/nps/park/fujihakone/index.html

This photo shows the huge tree roots visitors have to watch out for or risk twisting an ankle or worst.

Videos about Aokigahara can be found on YouTube, such as https://www.youtube.com/watch?v=4FDSdg09df8, but be forewarned that some are gruesomely graphic.

DOOR TO HELL (Turkmenistan)

This was once a gas field before the Soviets set it on fire. And it has been burning ever since, like an eternal flame. The sinister-looking fire looks like a Door to Hell or the Gates of Hell, which is pretty scary.

This fire was been burning furiously for more than five decades in the Karakum Desert. Efforts to curb the 230-foot-wide, 65-foot-deep inferno, known as the Darvaza Gas Crater, have been ongoing since it first ignited in 1971.

The most recent efforts have been led by Turkmenistan President Gurbanguly Berdymukhamedov, who has been urging experts, researchers, scientists, and government officials to "find a solution to extinguish this large burning crater. The Door to Hell is undeniably leaking valuable and environmentally harmful methane into the atmosphere.

Explorer George Kourounis was the first man (and the only one that I know of) to descend to the bottom of the pit in November 2013. He says that even seemingly logical fixes will probably prove futile.

"As I was digging into the ground [at the bottom of the crater] to gather these soil samples, fire would start coming out of the hole I just dug because it was a new path for the gas to come out of the crater," Kourounis says. "So even if you were to extinguish the fire and cover it up, there's a chance that the gas could still find its way out to the surface and all it would take is one spark to light it up again."

What caused this disaster? The origins of the fire are unclear. It is believed that the Soviets lit the collapsed area on fire to burn off the methane, assuming the blaze would last a day or two at the most. Local geologists, however, have argued the crater was formed in the late 1960s and didn't ignite until the 1980s.

However the mysterious fire began, it is obvious it is not going to be extinguished anytime soon. It is a spectacular sight but also a creepy one since it is a huge, continuous fire coming up out of the ground, which is why it is called the Door to Hell and also the Gates of Hell.

Some visitors actually camp overnight quite close to the Door to Hell.

FYI: Turkmenistan's is the second-most isolated county in the world with few tourists (North Korea is #1). Turkmenistan sits atop one of the largest natural gas deposits in the world and holds the world's fourth-largest known reserve of natural gas. The Door to Hell (aka "Gates of Hell) is near Darvaza).

MIYAKEJIMA ISLAND (Japan)

No, this isn't a scene out of a bad horror movie. To the contrary, it is just normal life on this Japanese island. Located 111 miles south of Tokyo, Miyakejima is a stratovolcano, which means the island is comprised of layers of lava and ash. Or to put it another way, the island is basically one big volcano.

Even though there have been numerous eruptions over the years, the main problem is the poisonous gases that leak up through the ground on a regular basis. Hence, the need for the gas masks and the reason for the island's nickname,

Gas-Mask Town.

Miyakejima is part of the Izu Islands, an archipelago in an area of the Pacific Ocean known as the "Devil's Sea." It is home to Mount Oyama, which is one of the most active volcanoes in all of Japan.

Since Mount Oyama releases poisonous sulfuric gases with hardly any warning, islanders and visitors must carry gas masks with them at all times. Sirens go off whenever unacceptable levels are reached and everyone must don their gas masks. This happens at all times of day, including the middle of the night.

The last eruption was in 2000. Everyone had to be evacuated after a series of eruptions created extremely dangerous levels of toxic gas. It was five years before residents were permitted to resume normal routines and eight years before flights to the area resumed.

Who would want to live here you may wonder? There are roughly 3,000 inhabitants at this time. They love their island and don't mind wearing the masks when necessary so they can continue to live here.

Visitors are allowed. While one-third of the island is off limits to residents and visitors, certain areas of the island are quite beautiful and the diving is very good around the island. There are hiking trails and bike paths, but it rains a lot here, so the trails and paths are often slippery. There is a black sand beach, a lighthouse, and botanical garden. Don't worry if you don't have a gas mask. They are for sale in most of the shops. www.japan-guide.com/e/e7300.html

FYI: Miyake-jima has a population of roughly 2,800. The main industries are agriculture and fishing. There have been thirteen significant eruptions with the worst volcanic activity occurring in 2000 when the entire island was evacuated. The population was nearly 4,000 prior to the evacuation, but more than 1,000 residents never returned to the island.

HOUSKA CASTLE (Czech Republic)

Houska Castle has a dark and intriguing history. This clifftop castle was originally constructed in the 13th century during the reign of Ottokar II of Bohemia. It was supposed to be an administrative hub for the king, but that makes no sense.

For one thing, the gothic-style castle has fake windows. Why there are no real windows in this massive castle? Why is there no kitchen? Why are there no stairs from the courtyard to the upper floors? Why does it have no source of water? And have you ever heard of a castle with no fortifications around it?

Even more strange is its location. If it

were meant to be an administrative hub for the king, it would be more centrally located. Instead, it was built atop a limestone cliff in a very remote area with nothing around it but swamps, mountains, and forests. So why build it here?

According to legend, Houska Castle was built over a hole in the ground that was so deep no one could see the bottom of it. It came to be known as the Gateway to Hell, but most locals call it the Hole to Hell. Legend has it that half-human, half-animal creatures used to crawl out of the pit at night and black-winged creatures used to attack locals and drag them down into the hole.

The castle was built over this hole to close the Gateway to Hell so that these demonic creatures could not escape. That's why there are no windows or kitchen or anything else you normally find in a castle.

This place is creepy, mysterious, and haunted. Many visitors claim they hear scratching, clawing, and screaming underneath the main floor of the castle where the sealed pit of demonic creatures is reportedly located.

Ghostly figures have been seen in the hallways. They disappear into thin air when someone tries to approach. Dead birds are often found in the castle's inner courtyard. It is unclear how they died or why it happens so regularly.

When the construction of the castle began, a village prisoner, who was sentenced to death, was offered a pardon if he agreed to be lowered by rope into the bottomless pit and report what he saw. The young man was lowered into the hole, and after a few minutes, he began screaming at the top of his lungs. He begged to be pulled back up. When the prisoner emerged from the hole he looked as if he had aged thirty years. His hair had turned white and the man could not be calmed down, so he was sent to an insane asylum for evaluation. He died two days later from unknown causes.

According to legend, the castle was even inhabited by a mad scientist. In 1639, the castle was occupied by a black magic practitioner, Oronto, who allegedly had a laboratory where he worked day and night concocting potions and elixirs for eternal life. He was killed by villagers who were afraid of him and his black magic.

Nazis occupied the castle during WWII. It is unknown what they were doing in the castle, but some of the theories include conducting experiments for paranormal weapons or a "breeding farm" for the Nazi's master race. Locals at the time reported strange lights and horrifying sounds coming from the castle.

Some say that many top Nazi officials, including SS leader Heinrich Himmler, attended dark ceremonies at Houska Castle in which they attempted to harness the power of Hell. Unfortunately, we will probably never know because all documents related to the castle at this time have been destroyed.

The demonic pit was covered up with stones and a chapel was built right on top of it. The chapel was dedicated to the Archangel Michael, who is known as the leader of God's army against the forces of evil.

Bottomless pit? Home to demonic creatures?

Castle Houska is thirty miles north of Prague. It is being restored by its current owners. It is open to visitors for an admission fee, which must be paid in cash. Some cool things to take note of inside the castle are the gothic chapel (supposedly built over the Gateway to Hell), some murals and frescoes, and a knights' drawing room.

https://www.visitczechrepublic.com/en-US/5ddaeb4e-1d37-4bfc-b349-c759b7527a3e/place/c-houska-castle

THE CLOWN MOTEL (Nevada, USA)

Lots of people think clowns are creepy. But even if you don't, the sight of 2,000 of them staring at you will probably creepy you out! There are clowns everywhere in this small motel. In fact, the motel boasts the largest private collection of clown figurines and memorabilia in America.

      The thirty-one room motel is next door to an old cemetery (self-guided walking tours are available) and is located in an old mining town. If none of this makes you run screaming, you should know that every guest room features three pieces of "clown art." The murals alone will give most folks nightmares! And did I mention the clown gift shop?

**FYI: The Clown Motel has been dubbed
"America's Scariest Motel!"**

The motel is in the middle of the desert, miles from anywhere. Also, it is reportedly haunted by friendly ghosts, especially rooms 108, 111, 210, and 214. Guests to the motel have reported odd laughter throughout the corridors. One man claimed to wake up to a full-bodied clown apparition. For housekeeper Andrea Selig, it's been no laughing matter. "When I come in here I just get horrible anxiety. I literally feel like there's somebody with me in this room." She also claims to have seen apparitions in the neighboring cemetery. Renowned ghost investigating group, Ghost Adventure, was able to capture EVP, as well as video of a clown doll's hand moving.

The Clown Motel is located halfway between Reno and Las Vegas at 521 Main Street in Tonopah, NV. Tonopah Ghost Walks are offered during the summer months. Believe it or not, the motel books up during summer months, so be sure to make reservations. www.theclownmotelusa.com

Tonopah Cemetery

 **FYI: Tonopah is an unincorporated town located at the junction of U.S. Routes 6 and 95. It has a population of 2,100. This historic town began with the discovery of gold and silver by prospector Jim Butler on May 19, 1900. When Butler went in search of his missing burro he found him and the second richest silver strike in Nevada history. In 1905, a "plague" (later discovered to be pneumonia) swept through Tonopah killing 56 residents. Also, many of Tonopah's earliest silver mine workers who died in the Belmont Mine Fire of 1911 are buried here.**

TERRANCE ZEPKE
Series Reading Order
& Guide

Series List

Most Haunted Series

Spookiest Series

Terrance Talks Travel Series

Cheap Travel Series

Weird & Wonderful Travel Series

Strange Series

Stop Talking Series

Books & Guides for the Carolinas Series

& More Books by Terrance Zepke

≈

Introduction

Terrance Zepke studied Journalism at the University of Tennessee and later received a Master's degree in Mass Communications from the University of South Carolina. She studied parapsychology at the renowned Rhine Research Center.

Zepke spends much of her time happily traveling around the world but always returns home to the Carolinas where she lives part-time in both states. She has written hundreds of articles and more than fifty books. She is the host of *Terrance Talks Travel: Über Adventures*. Additionally, this award-winning and best-selling author has been featured in many publications and programs, such as NPR, CNN, *The Washington Post,* Associated Press, Travel with Rick Steves, Around the World, *Publishers Weekly,* World Travel & Dining with Pierre Wolfe, *San Francisco Chronicle*, Good Morning Show, *Detroit Free Press*, The Learning Channel, and The Travel Channel.

When she's not investigating haunted places, searching for pirate treasure, or climbing lighthouses, she is most likely packing for her next adventure to some far flung place, such as Reykjavik or Kwazulu Natal. Some of her favorite adventures include piranha fishing on the Amazon, shark cage diving in South Africa, hiking Peru's Inca Trail, camping in the Himalayas, dog-sledding in the Arctic Circle, and a gorilla safari in the Congo.

Sign up for *Terrance Talks Travel* blog for free downloadable travel reports, adventure travel tips, travel news, and more at www.terrancetalkstravel.com.

You can follow her travel show, **TERRANCE TALKS TRAVEL: ÜBER ADVENTURES on** www.blogtalkradio.com/terrancetalkstravel or subscribe to it at **iTunes** or **Amazon Podcasts.**

Warning: Listening to this show could lead to a spectacular South African safari, hot-air ballooning over the Swiss Alps, Disney Adventures, and Tornado Tours!

MOST HAUNTED SERIES

A Ghost Hunter's Guide to the Most Haunted Places in America
A Ghost Hunter's Guide to the Most Haunted Houses in America
A Ghost Hunter's Guide to the Most Haunted Hotels & Inns in America
A Ghost Hunter's Guide to the Most Haunted Historic Sites in America
A Ghost Hunter's Guide to the Most Haunted Places in the World

The Ghost Hunter's MOST HAUNTED Box Set (3 in 1): Discover America's Most Haunted Destinations

MOST HAUNTED and SPOOKIEST Sampler Box Set: Featuring *A GHOST HUNTER'S GUIDE TO THE MOST HAUNTED PLACES IN AMERICA* and *SPOOKIEST CEMETERIES*

≈

SPOOKIEST SERIES

Spookiest Lighthouses
Spookiest Battlefields
Spookiest Cemeteries
Spookiest Objects
Spookiest Military Bases

Spookiest Box Set (3 in 1): Discover America's Most Haunted Destinations

≈

TERRANCE TALKS TRAVEL SERIES

Terrance Talks Travel: A Pocket Guide to South Africa
Terrance Talks Travel: A Pocket Guide to African Safaris
Terrance Talks Travel: A Pocket Guide to Adventure Travel
Terrance Talks Travel: A Pocket Guide to Florida Keys (including Key West & The Everglades)
Terrance Talks Travel: The Quirky Tourist Guide to Key West
Terrance Talks Travel: The Quirky Tourist Guide to Cape Town
Terrance Talks Travel: The Quirky Tourist Guide to Reykjavik
Terrance Talks Travel: The Quirky Tourist Guide to Charleston, South Carolina
Terrance Talks Travel: The Quirky Tourist Guide to Ushuaia
Terrance Talks Travel: The Quirky Tourist Guide to Antarctica
Terrance Talks Travel: The Quirky Tourist Guide to Machu Picchu & Cuzco (Peru)

Terrance Talks Travel: A Pocket Guide to Uganda and Rwanda
Terrance Talks Travel: A Pocket Guide to New Zealand
Terrance Talks Travel: A Pocket Guide to Edinburgh (Scotland)
Terrance Talks Travel: The Quirky Tourist Guide to Kathmandu (Nepal) & The Himalayas
Terrance Talks Travel: The Quirky Tourist Guide to Marrakesh (Morocco)
Terrance Talks Travel: The Quirky Tourist Guide to Amsterdam
Terrance Talks Travel: The Quirky Tourist Guide to Queensland
Terrance Talks Travel: The Quirky Tourist Guide to Sydney
Terrance Talks Travel: The Quirky Tourist Guide to Savannah, Georgia
Terrance Talks Travel: The Quirky Tourist Guide to Myrtle Beach, South Carolina
Terrance Talks Travel: The Quirky Tourist Guide to the Outer Banks, North Carolina
Terrance Talks Travel: The Quirky Tourist Guide to Wilmington & the Cape Fear Coast, North Carolina

African Safari Box Set: *A Pocket Guide to South Africa* and *A Pocket Guide to African Safaris*

CHEAP TRAVEL SERIES

How to Cruise Cheap!

How to Fly Cheap!

How to Travel Cheap!

How to Travel FREE or Get Paid to Travel!

CHEAP TRAVEL SERIES (4 IN 1) BOX SET

≈

WEIRD & WONDERFUL TRAVELS SERIES

Weirdest Museums in the World
Weirdest Tourist Attractions in the World
Weirdest Accommodations in the World
(Coming Soon!)

≈

STRANGE SERIES

The Most Cursed Places in the World
The Creepiest Places in the World

≈

STOP TALKING SERIES

Stop Talking & Start Writing Your Book
Stop Talking & Start Publishing Your Book
Stop Talking & Start Selling Your Book

Stop Talking & Start Writing Your Book Series
(3 in 1) Box Set

≈

BOOKS & GUIDES FOR THE CAROLINA SERIES & MORE BOOKS BY TERRANCE ZEPKE

Lighthouses of the Carolinas for Kids
Pirates of the Carolinas for Kids
Ghosts of the Carolinas for Kids
Ghosts of the Carolina Coasts
The Best Ghost Tales of South Carolina
Ghosts & Legends of the Carolina Coasts
The Best Ghost Tales of North Carolina
Pirates of the Carolinas
Coastal South Carolina: Welcome to the Lowcountry
Coastal North Carolina: Its Enchanting Islands, Towns & Communities
Lighthouses of the Carolinas: A Short History & Guide
Lowcountry Voodoo: Tales, Spells & Boo Hags
Ghosts of Savannah
How To Train Your Puppy or Dog Using Three Simple Strategies

*Fiction books written under a pseudonym.

≈

Message from the Author

The primary purpose of this guide is to introduce you to some titles you may not have known about. The great thing about my book series is that they do not have to be read in any order and you don't have to read all the books in the series—only the ones that intrigue you! Another reason for this short guide is to let you know all the ways you can connect with me. Authors love to hear from readers. We truly appreciate you more than you'll ever know. Don't forget that you can also listen to my travel show, **Terrance Talks Travel: Über Adventures** on Blog Talk Radio, Amazon Podcasts, and iTunes. Sign up for my travel blog *,Terrance Talks Travel,* at www.terrancetalkstravel.com.

Terrance

P.S. I would like to ask you to take a couple of minutes to share your feedback about any of my books you have read by posting a short review (just a sentence or two) on your favorite bookseller's site so that other readers might discover the title too. Authors appreciate readers more than you realize and we dearly love and depend upon your good reviews. Thank you!

FREE REPORTS!

Visit http://terrancezepke.com/shop/ to download dozens of free reports, such as:

*Best Ghost Walks in America

*Wonders of the World: Ten Places Travelers Need to See

 *Weird & Wonderful Worldwide Celebrations of the Dead

*Perfect Places to Celebrate Christmas

*Most Popular Tourist Attractions in America

*Twelve Best Places in the U.S. to Enjoy Autumn & Fall Colors

*Discover the #1 Travel Ailment, Who is Most Likely to Get It (Surprise!), and How to Avoid it

...and much more!

See the next page for a sneak peek of *SPOOKIEST OBJECTS:* Discover the World's Most Haunted Objects

(Book #4 SPOOKIEST SERIES)

Now available from Safari Publishing

Royal Chairs of Belcourt

Location: Newport, Rhode Island

Origin: The house was built in 1894; the chairs once belonged to French royalty, but the date of origin is unknown.

Visitor Information: The house was sold by Mrs. Tinney in 2012. It is privately owned and not open to the public. However, special seasonal tours are given, such as their candlelight ghost tours during the fall.

657 Bellevue Avenue. Newport, Rhode Island 02840

www.belcourt.com.

About The Haunted Object: Newport is one of the oldest towns in America, dating back to

1690. It is home to some of the wealthiest
families in America, which means there are
many mansions here. One such mansion is
Belcourt Castle. After three years of
construction, the sixty-room, three-story,
50,000-square foot castle was completed.

This is a spectacular place to have such
humble beginnings. The "Belcourt" began as a
hunting lodge. The original plan called for one
bedroom and one bathroom. There was no
kitchen, but there was a huge stable and sleeping
quarters for all the servants. Reportedly, he had
thirty horses and thirty servants in the early days
at Belcourt. His racing horses were given only
the best. They each had comfortable stalls and
slept on fine linens imported from Ireland.

Somehow this simple plan ballooned into
a 50,000 square-foot edifice that included sixty
rooms. It was designed by renowned architect
Richard M. Hunt in a Louis XIII French
Renaissance style and required 300 European
craftsmen to build it. A kitchen was eventually
built but not in the house as Oliver was terribly
afraid that a fire might break out in the kitchen

and destroy the home. He built the kitchen in another building and food was delivered by carriage to the main house. There are tunnels that extended from the house to the kitchen so that servants could easily go back and forth.

It cost three million dollars and three and a half years to complete (1891 – 1894). The price tag is equivalent to over seventy million today. No wonder ghosts choose to linger here!

This may seem extravagant for a hunting retreat, but not to its owner. Oliver Belmont was born on November 12, 1858. His father was a banker and one of the richest men in the world. At 24, Oliver married Sara Swan Whiting, but the pair divorced that same year. Sara gave birth to a baby girl soon after the divorce became final. Oliver never saw his daughter, who died in her 20s.

Oliver Hazard Perry Belmont inherited sixty million dollars in 1890, so money was no object. In addition to being very wealthy, the bachelor had many other appealing qualities. He was a graduate of Annapolis Naval Academy, had served one term as a Congressman, belonged to all the right social clubs, and had lots of interesting hobbies.

Oliver eventually remarried. Of all the women he could have had, Oliver ended up marrying his best friend's ex-wife, Anna Vanderbilt, less than one year after the divorce. She was responsible for many renovations in the house. Reportedly, she had the Grand Staircase moved four times before the workmen refused to do it anymore. When Oliver died in 1908, Anna threw herself into politics, especially women's' rights. It seemed she liked to live well too. At one point, she owned nine estates.

She chose her favorite for retirement, a chateau in France. She lived there until her death in 1933. She had a good life, living to a ripe old age of 80. She would have lived longer had she not suffered certain injuries during a carriage accident. She was buried next to Oliver in the Belmont family mausoleum in New York.

Oliver's nineteen-year-old nephew, August Belmont IV inherited Belcourt. But it ended up in the possession of Oliver's last surviving brother, who sold it in 1940. Belcourt was no longer in the Belmont family for the first time in its history. And it changed ownership several more times until 1956 when it was bought by Harold B. Tinney. The Tinney family drove by the vacant mansion and knew immediately that they wanted it. They bought it at the bargain price of $25,000.

The following year it became Belcourt Castle and a public museum. The Tinney family appreciated the beauty of the mansion. They made many renovations to the rundown property and delighted in furnishing it with spectacular antiques and works of art from nearly three dozen countries.

The home has many remarkable features. The library, which was added by Alva Belmont, has four secret doors. The grand staircase is hand-carved, which took hundreds of European craftsmen three years to complete. Other noteworthy features include a huge Russian chandelier made with 13,000 crystal prisms. It is surrounded by eight smaller crystal chandeliers. There is an oval Versailles dining room ceiling that is hand sculptured. French Empire style columns, mirrored doors, and mirrored shutters create a spectacular effect. When open, they overlook the ocean. The most spectacular room and the most haunted room in the house is the ballroom.

Or should I say that the most haunted objects are in the ballroom. The most famous are a pair of salt chairs. No one is permitted to sit in them. Those who try are violently ejected by an unseen presence. Some have been thrown as far as seven or eight feet away. They are thrown up into the air and then propelled forward. But before they are thrown out of the chair, they say they feel like they are sitting on something— or someone. Just touching them supposedly results in a strange sensation akin to getting shocked. Many have reported feeling queasy as soon as they are within close range of the chairs. Some feel suddenly cold as soon as they are near the chairs.

Salt chairs were once custom designed for royalty. Only kings were permitted to sit in them. A compartment was built in the chair that held a commodity once prized more than gold or jewels—salt! The king would present a bag of salt to esteemed visitors, such as foreign dignitaries. At that time, it was considered to be the finest gift the king could bestow. Perhaps the spirit of one of these kings is trying to protect his possession.

The entire ballroom is believed to be haunted by lingering spirits. One psychic claims there are fifteen lingering spirits in this room. Visitors and family members have reported:

*spooky feeling, as if being watched

*footsteps

*disembodied male voice saying "Get out!"

*strange shadows are seen sometimes in one corner of the room

*lights mysteriously going on

*screams

The screams are believed to be connected to a suit of armor that is in the ballroom. A suit of armor has a helmet that is cracked. According to the legend, the crack occurred when a spear pierced the warrior's eye. It is believed that he died a slow, painful death. His anguished screams are heard on rare occasions. But that's not all. There is a mirror in the music room that is haunted. People sometimes report their reflection is moving even though they are not! They describe their reflections as "vibrating."

The Tinneys placed a monk statue in their bedroom. The Tinneys saw a monk at the foot of their bed on occasion. Later, the statue was moved to the first floor near the ladies rest room. Some tour guides and visitors have reported seeing someone wearing a brown robe and a hood near the rest room. One tour guide saw it disappear into the rest room. She followed to let him know that he was going into the wrong bathroom, but she found no one in the rest room! After the psychic's visit, the monk statue was moved into the chapel. The psychic said that the monk had communicated his wishes to her while she was visiting. The monk entity has not been seen since the statue was moved to the chapel.

There have been sightings and paranormal activity in other parts of the house. Some believe Donald Tinney is one of the lingering spirits, unable even in death to leave his beloved home.

There have been ghost investigations of the property, including SyFy's *Ghost Hunters*. A thorough investigation captured evidence of paranormal activity.

Index

Made in the USA
Columbia, SC
22 February 2024

32190693R00104